MARC THIROUIN

Marc is well versed in projects related to both art and fashion. He is based in Paris, but has collected influential ideas and impressions from his years in highly contrasting Norway. His photos reflect his inner peculiar world, and invite the spectator to join an emotional voyage.

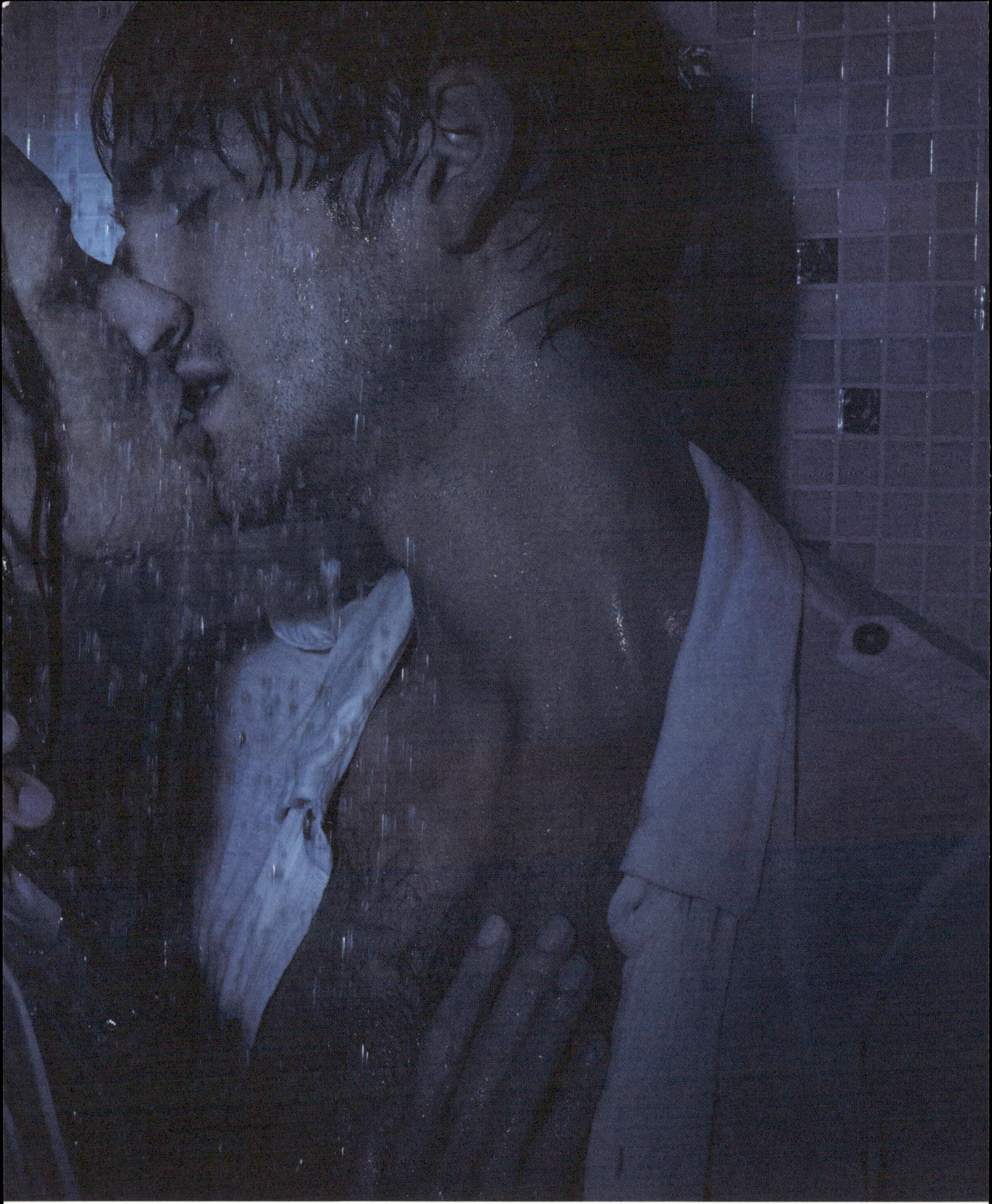

"We seek each other out...
Dead keen on him, she fascinates me,
I fly off, he melts, she lights me up.
I dive in, he touches me -
unexpected.

I distract him, she reassures me, he
protects me.
I unveil; we both hide, stalling...
I inhale him, evaporating, I adore
her."

Emotion is what Marc Thirouin attempts to immortalise here on paper, through a series of photographic stories and vignettes.

The "French Kiss", when dissected, is not just the romantic kiss of lovers but the very symbol of an emotion. A kiss is not merely an exchange between two partners exploring each other, softly biting or grazing each other's lips and tongue; it also answers a primary need from which "chemical essences" emanate. Ephemeral but oh-so-longed-for essences, who wouldn't love to capture them in order to feel their effects forever? It is this notion we have attempted to freeze in time.

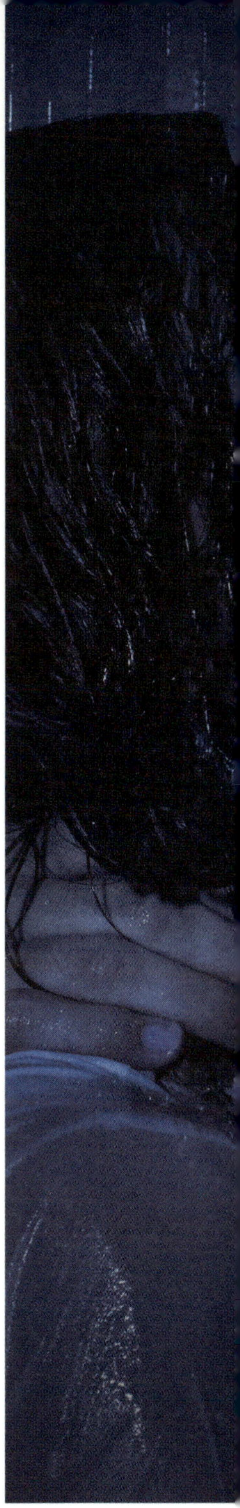

To keep true to the idea of instantaneity and to the fragrance of its emotional power, the seventeen images have been staged using real couples. Every element of design then reinforces the emotion at play. Here the intensity of the light is veiled, lending more power to the intimate and at times secretive state of the lived moment- the characters are trapped in the very half-light that reveals them.

This is photographic poetry, glimpsed in fantastical and velvety glimmers, an appetising prelude acting as emotional lever, where each one of us is free to imagine and make ours the emerging story...
Emotion is indeed a universal story.

Amandine Vignon for Marc Thirouin

For this project, the photographer chose to collaborate with Amandine Vignon, Arts & Mode's artistic director. Together they decrypted their own personal sense of "the French Kiss". In the last image, the conclusion to their work, the two protagonists themselves took centre stage.

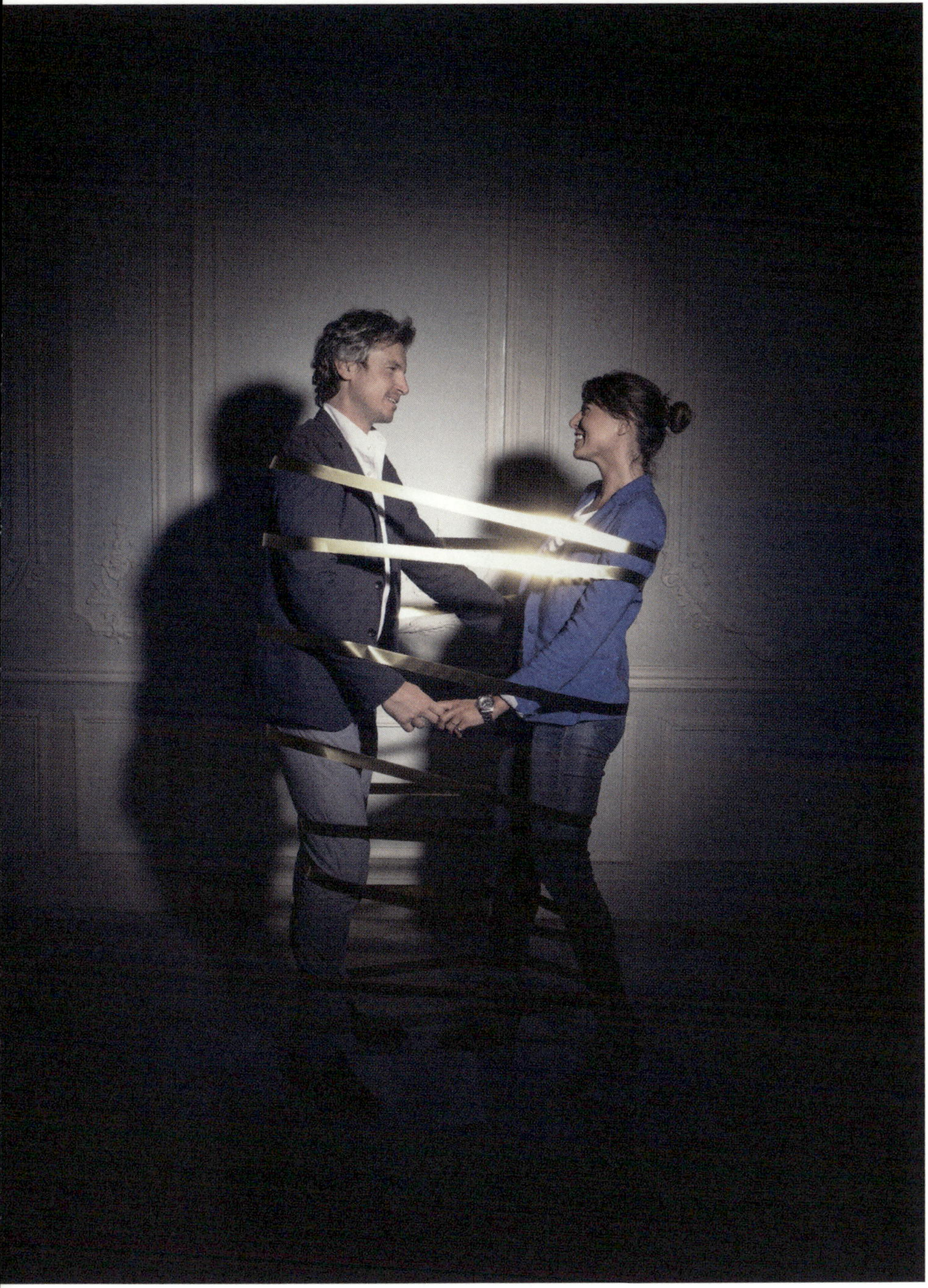

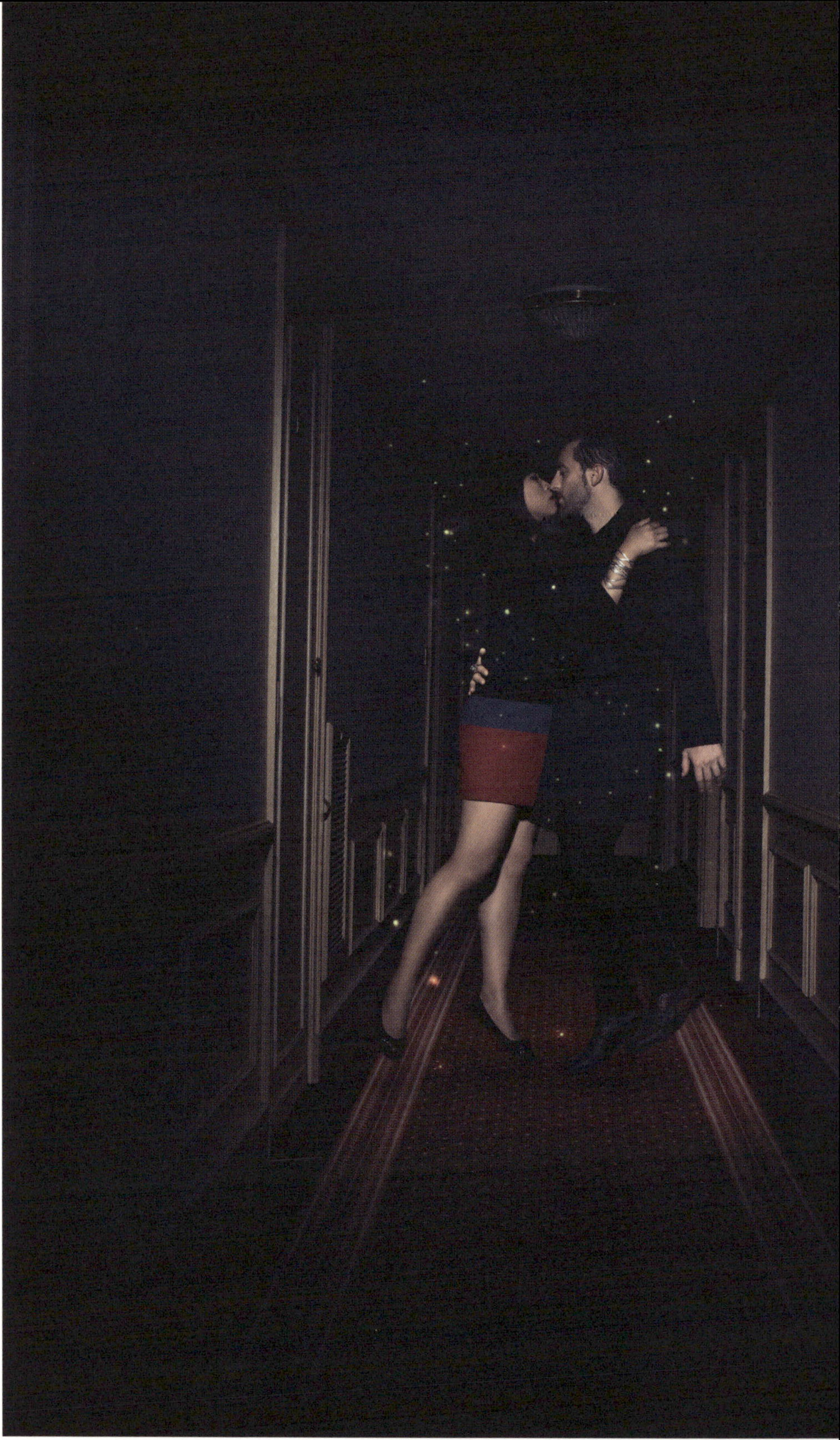

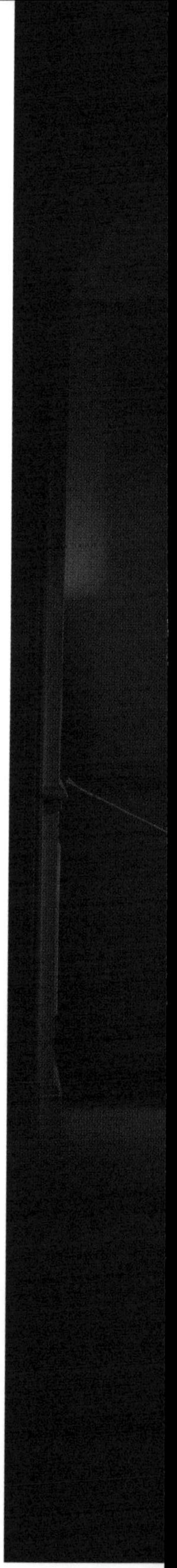

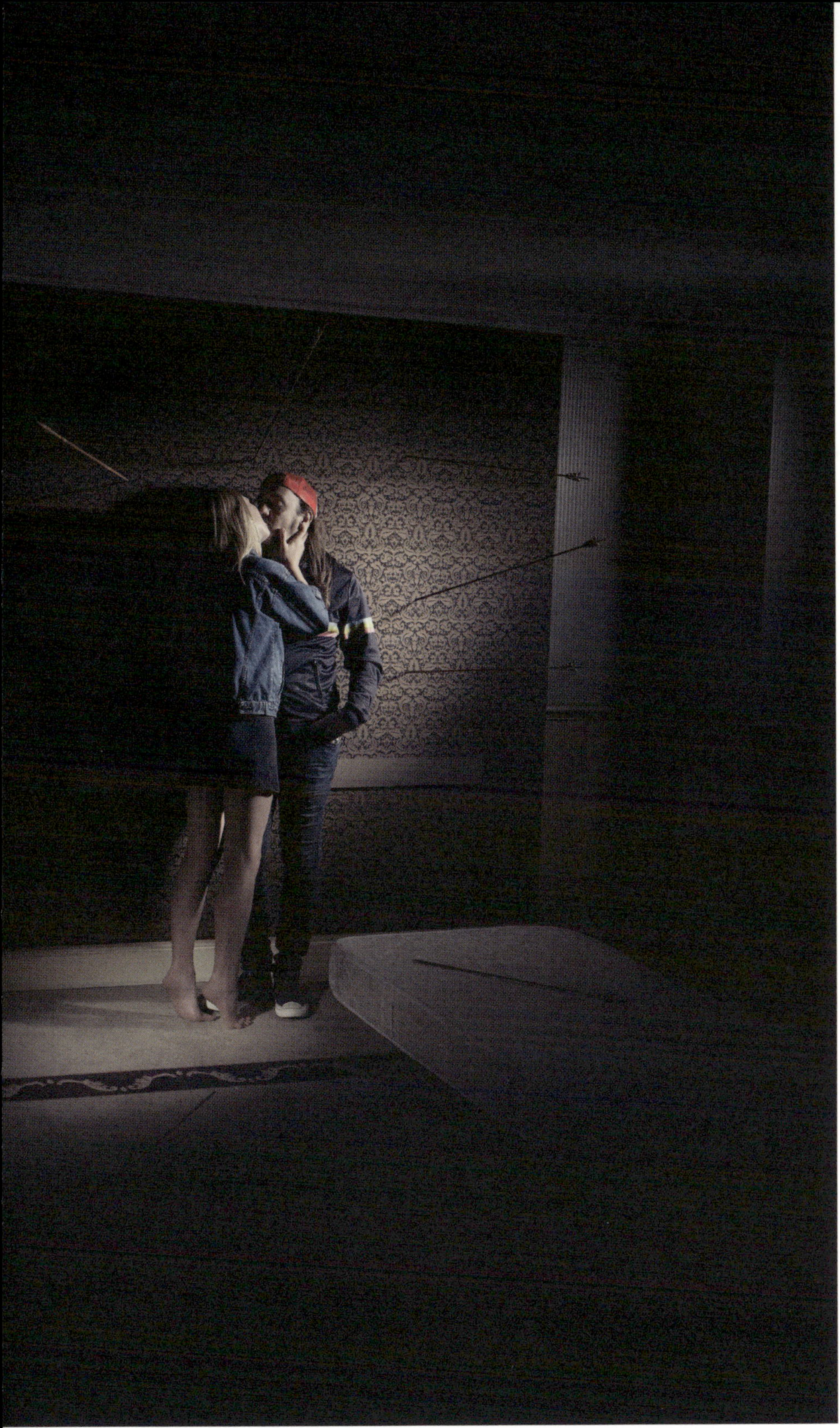

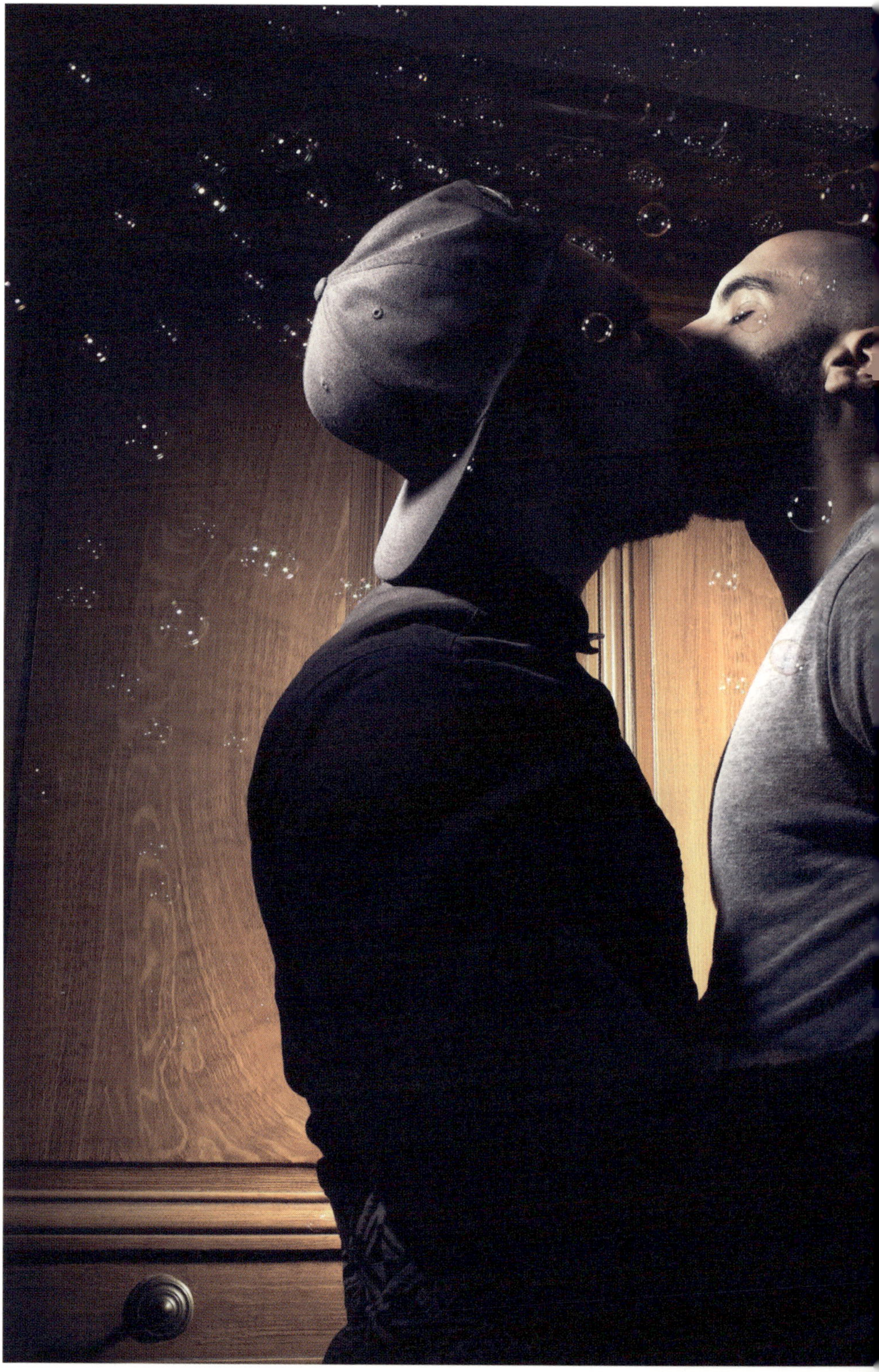

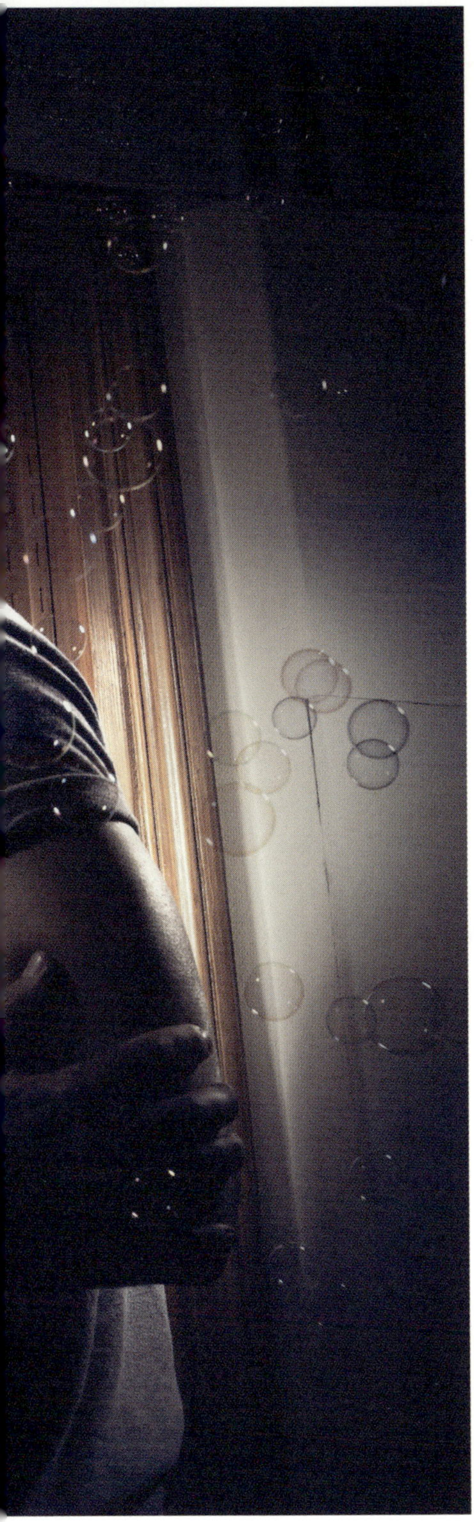

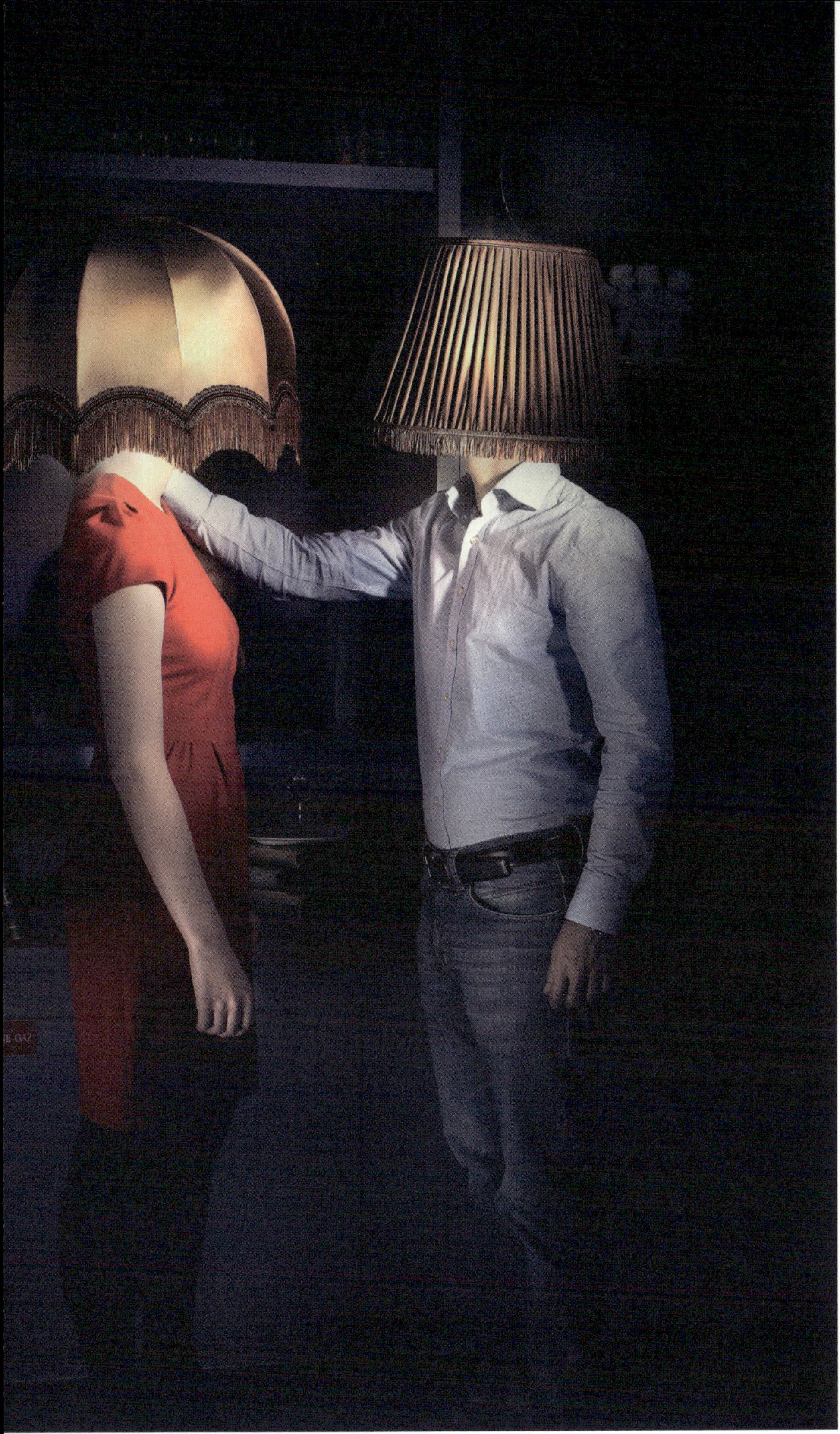

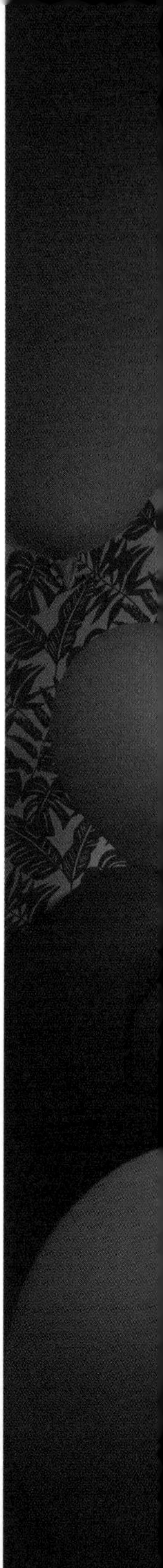

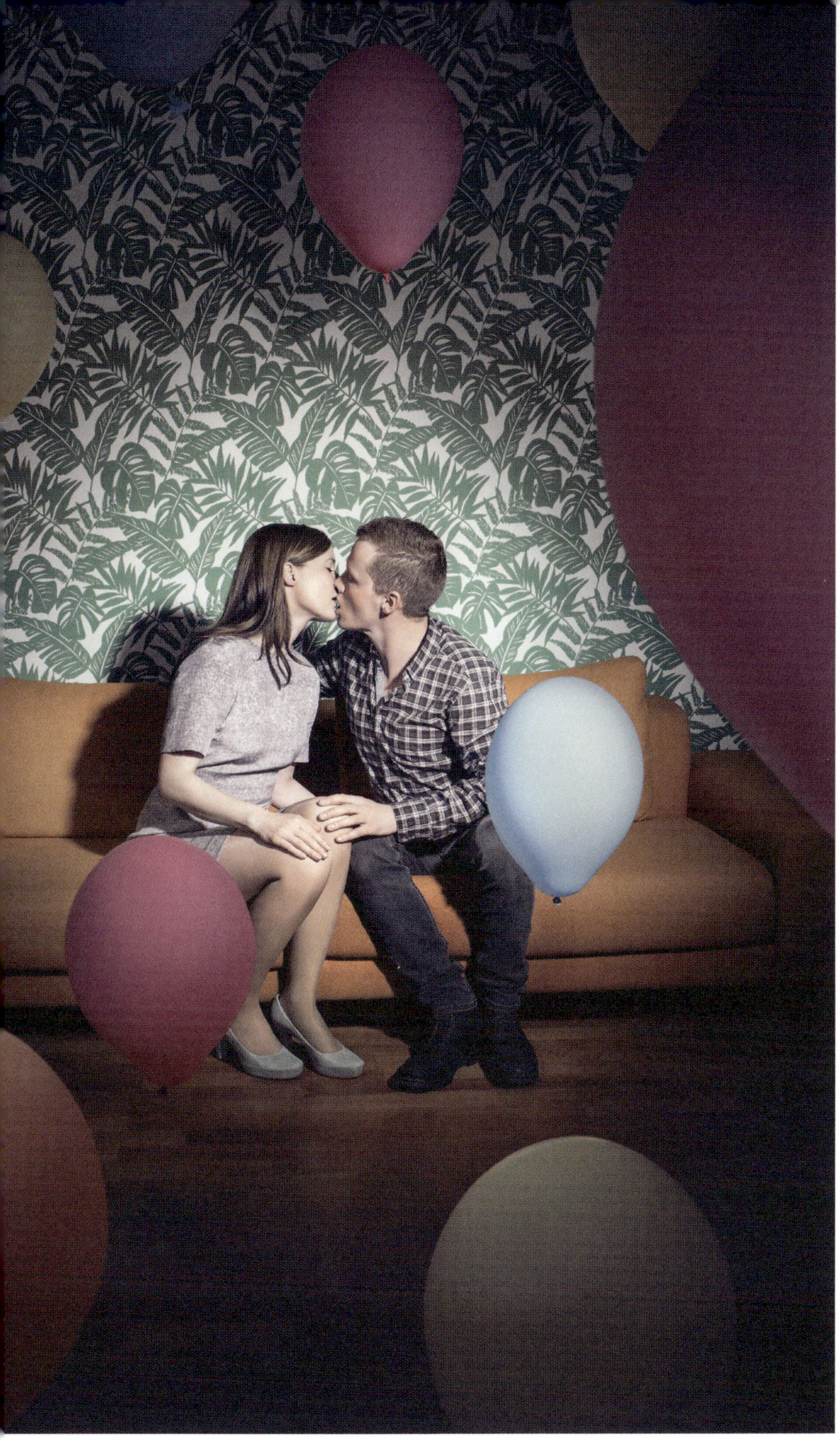

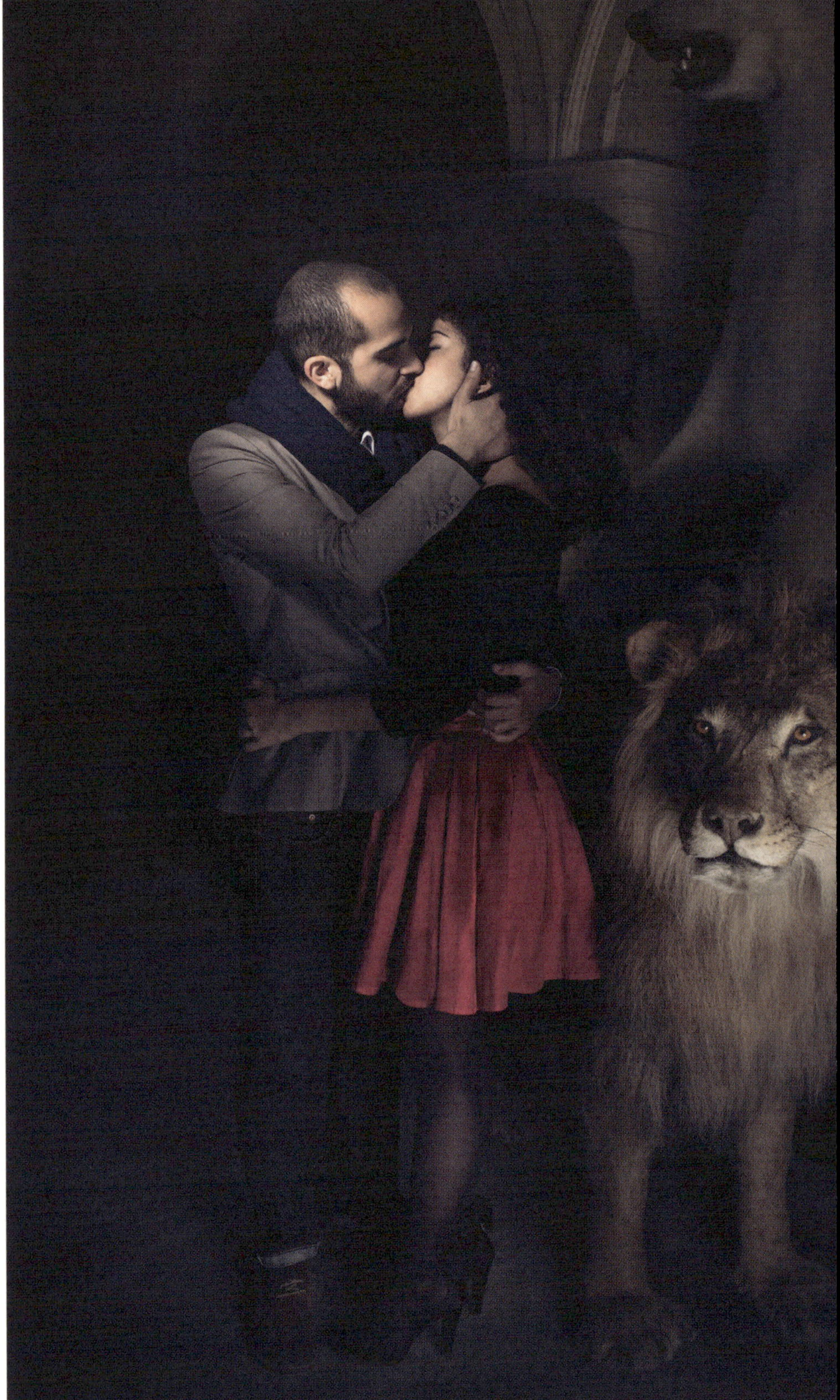

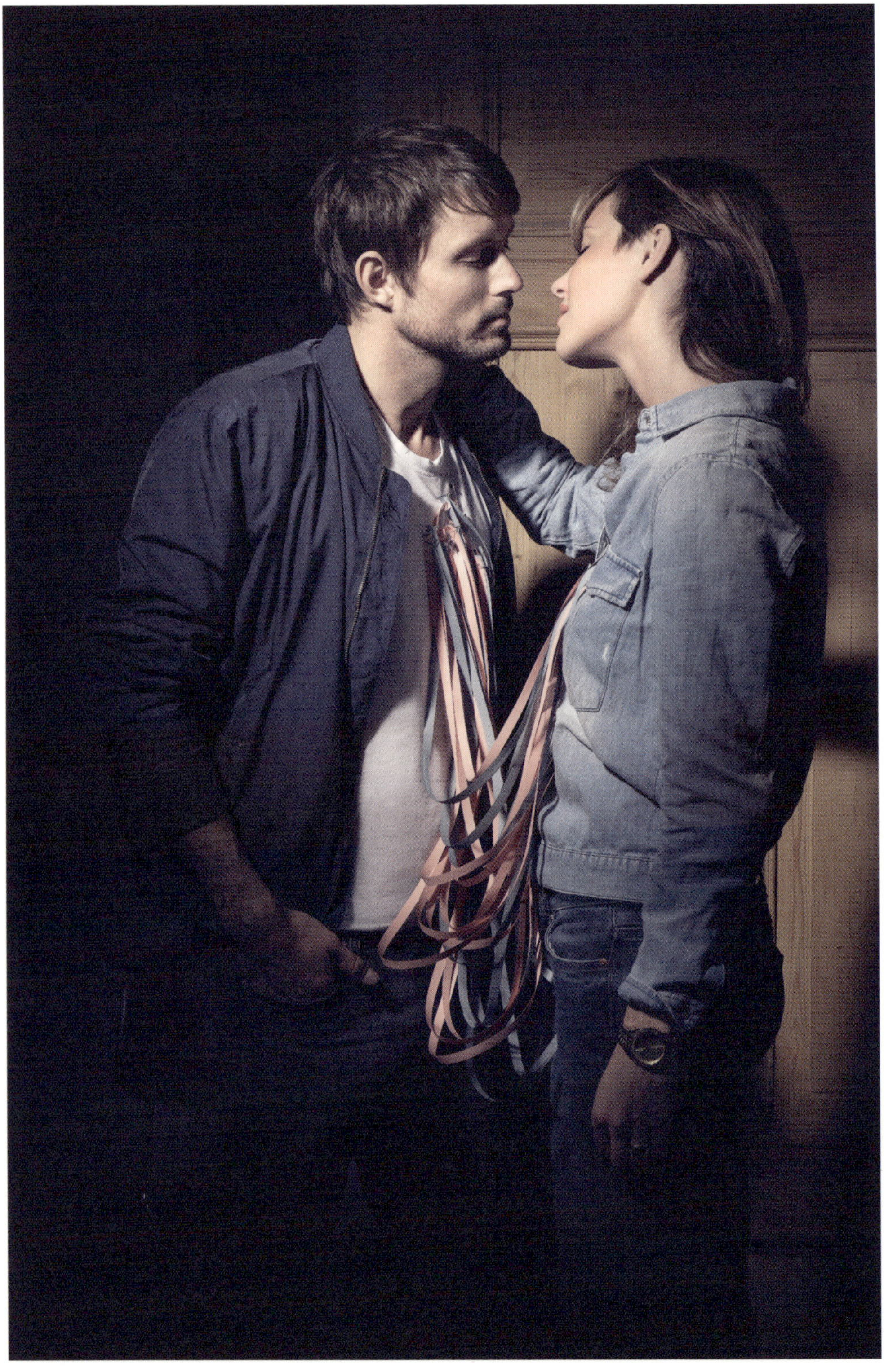

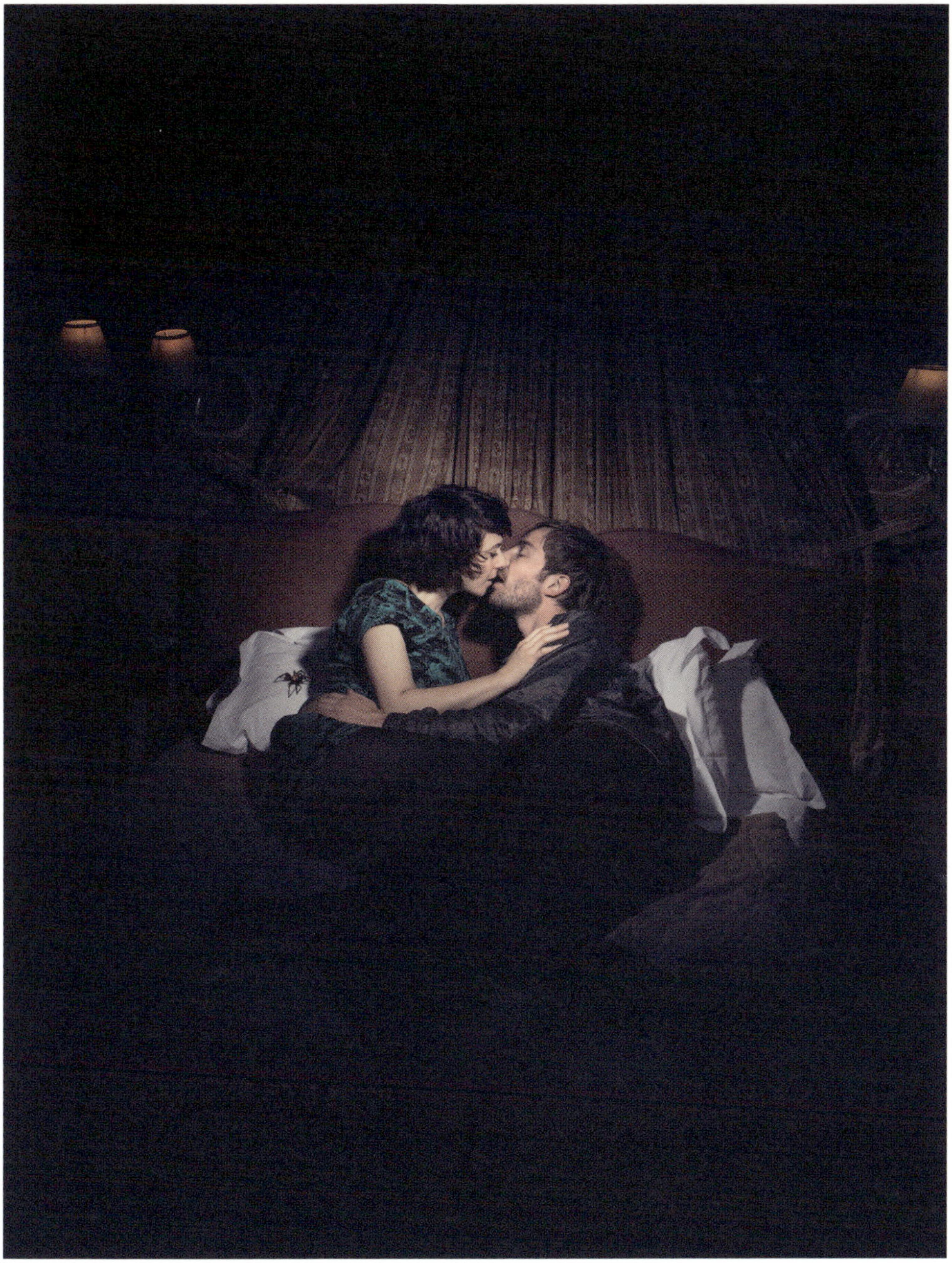

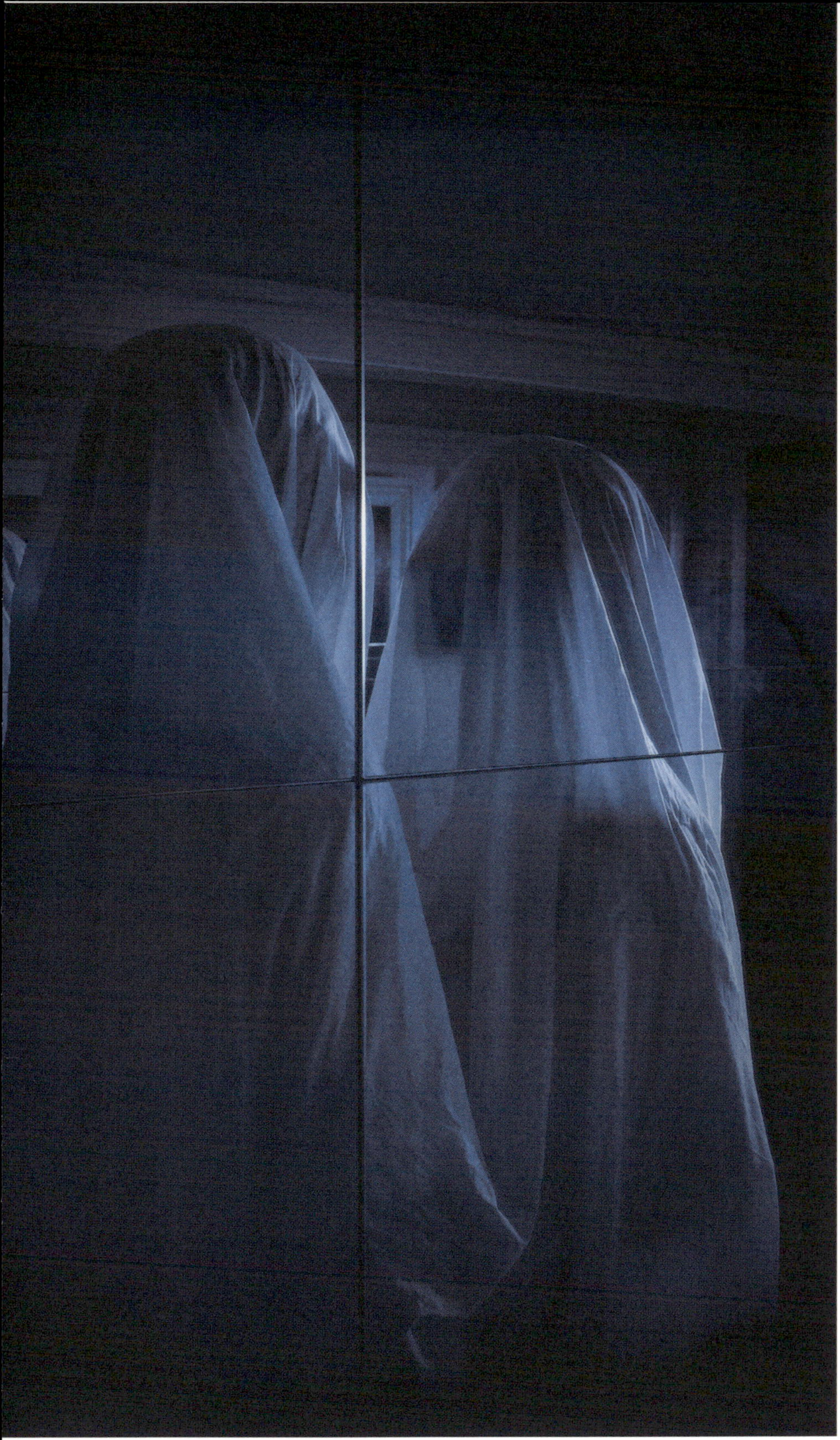

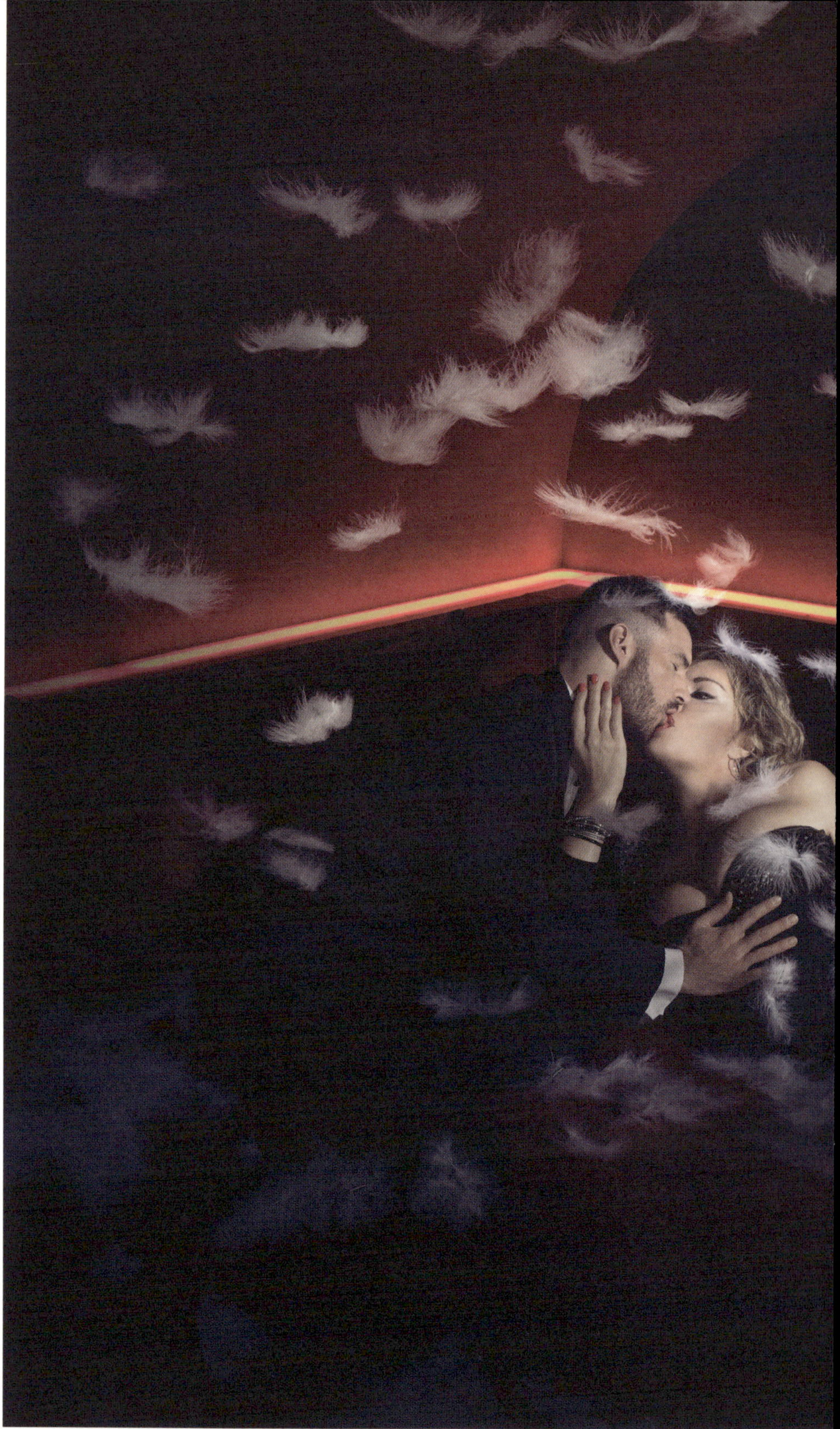

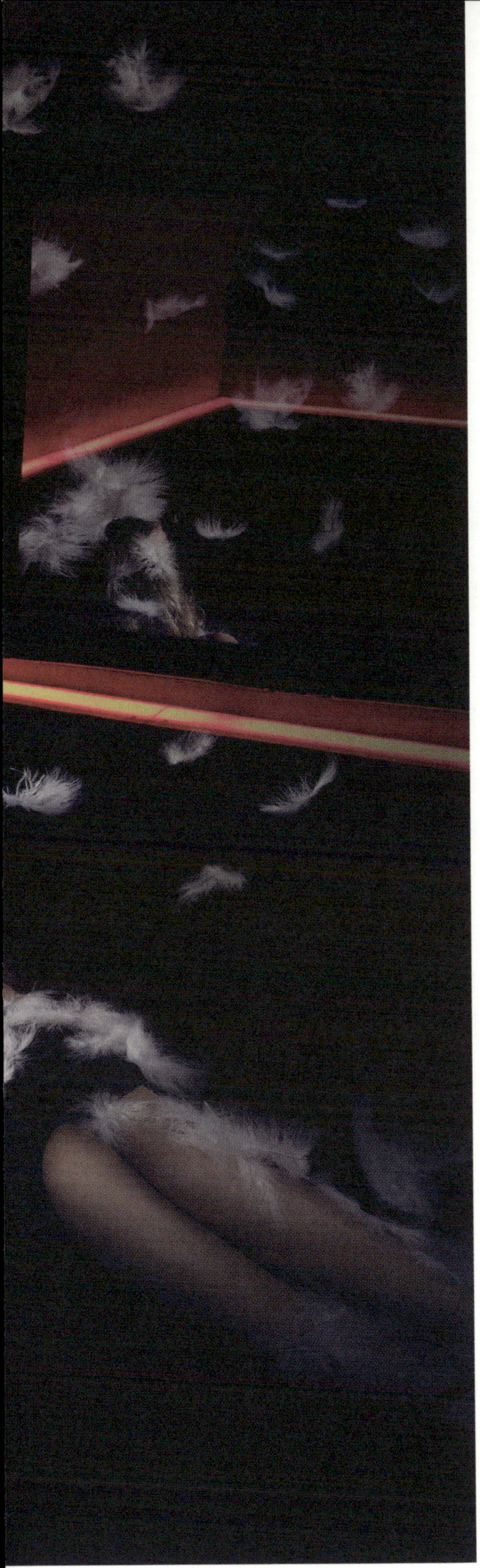

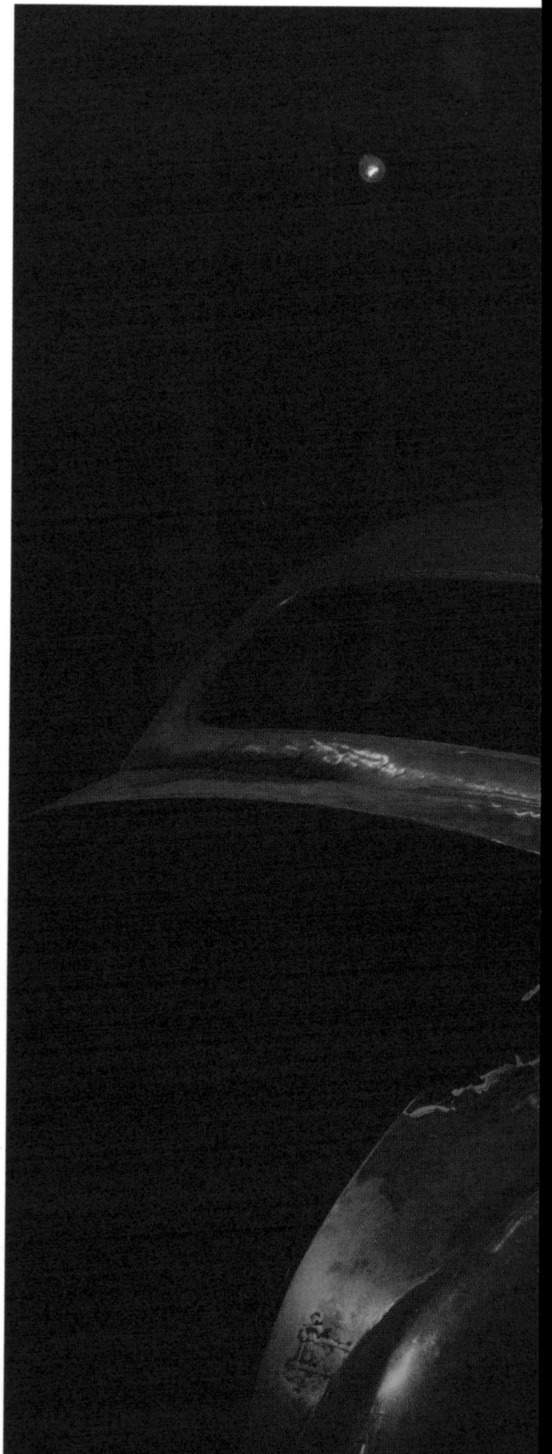

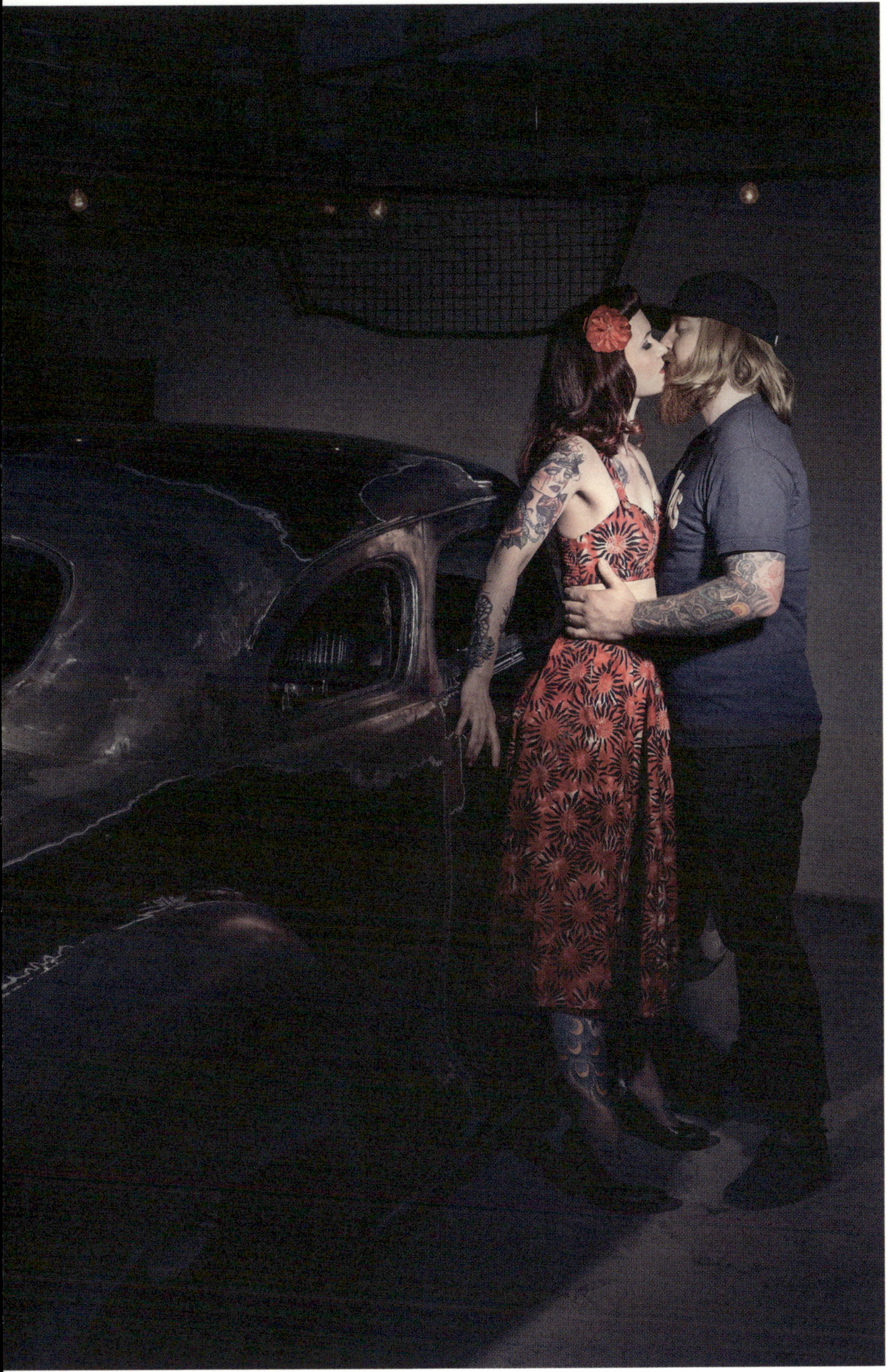

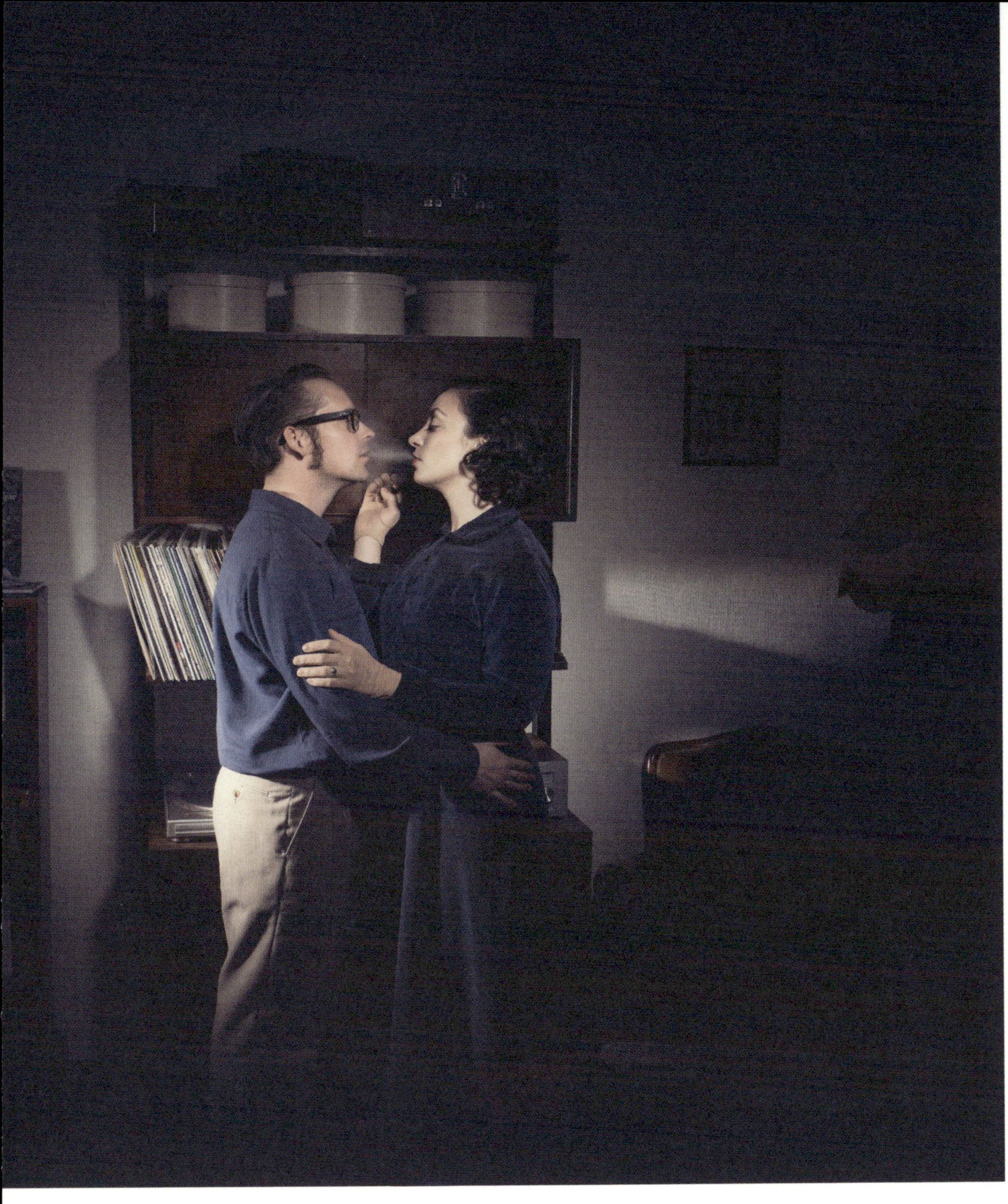

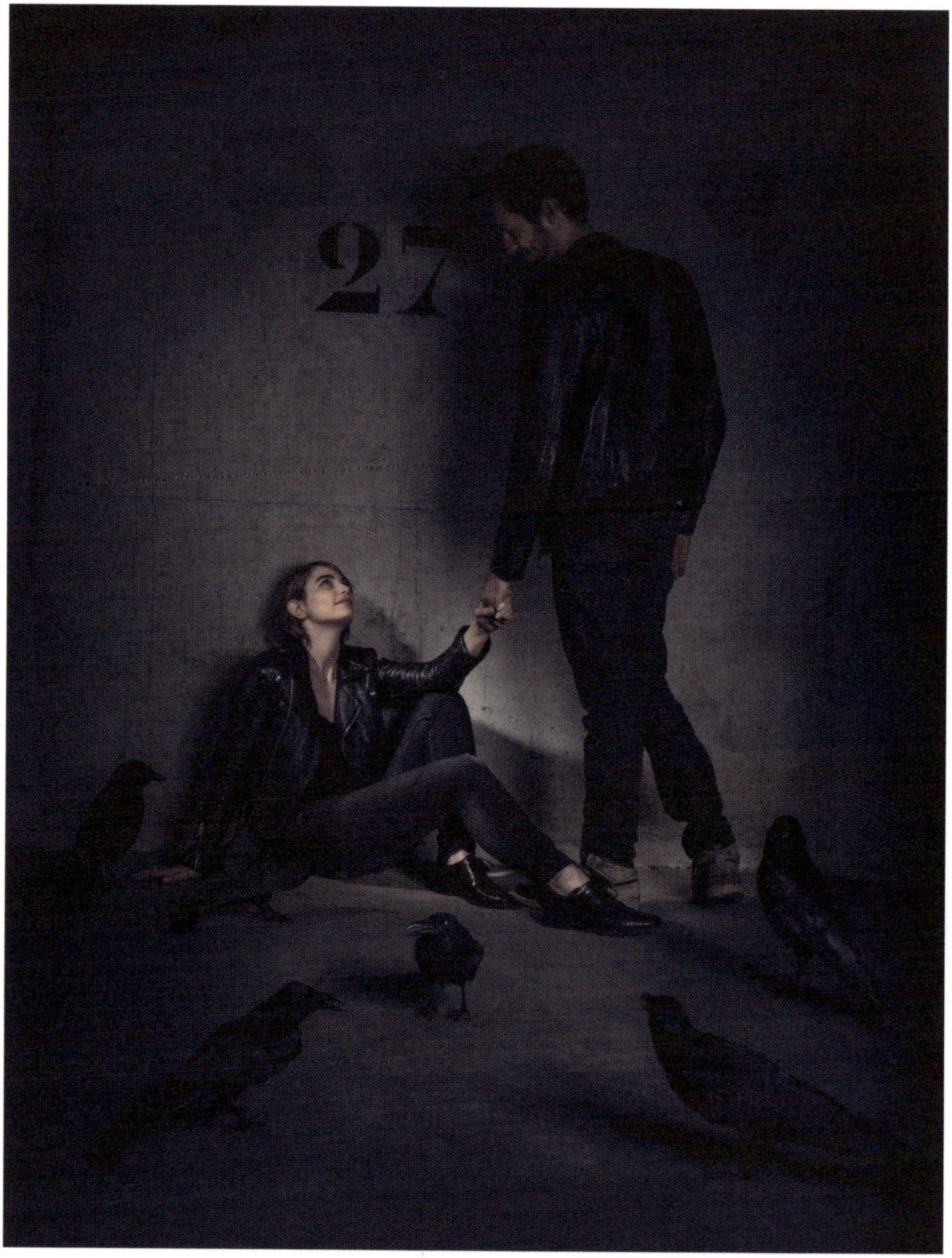
27

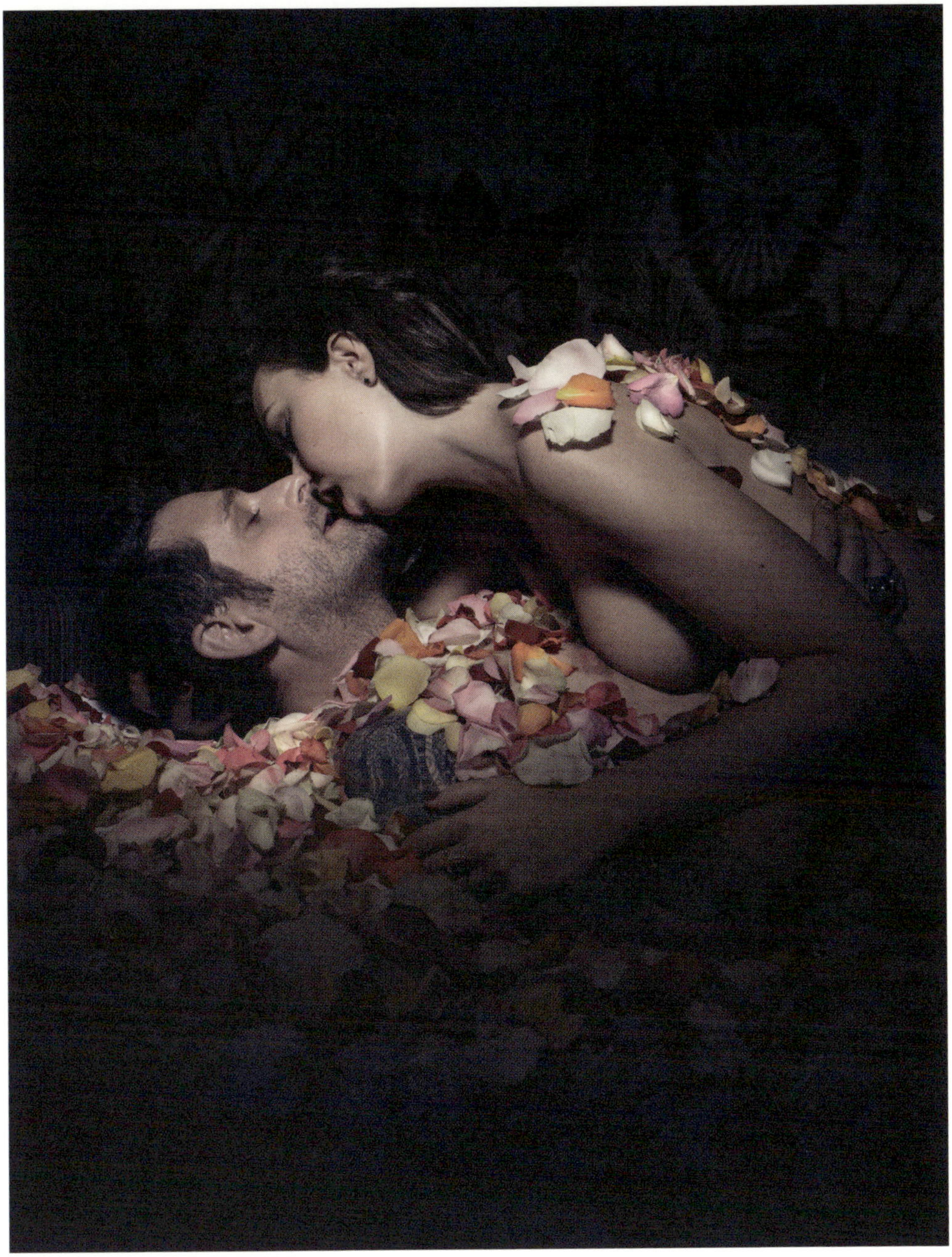

Here it is frozen. Like a flash portrait suspended out of time, engraved, stamped and branded- with hot iron at times- the chemical essence travels through from head to toe. The frame captures and encircles the emanations of its lyrical magnetism to try and retain it, like the canvas frames the painting in its ever-undulating race, towards emotion.

I dedicated this løve project to Yolanda Gennari, Elfi, Cristina & Christian, Jacques & Dany.

Yéta, Mélanie Pain, Oliver Smith, Servane Magnan, Emmanuel Duverrière, Guillaume Trouvé, Magdalena Ptounche, Claire Denimal, Edouard Bécret, Marion Blanchard-Gantier, Nicolas Blanchard, Gabrielle Nguyen, Christophe Ruggi, Edouard Tardu, Léa Fouet, Samy Jo, Justino Esteves, Erik Naevestad, Marion Naevestad, Thomas Halmø, Mari Aam, Natasha Meland, Gunnar Møtland, Sarah Telmat, Travers Wesley, Tonya, Dehaynin Arnaud, Pauline Käh, Clément Saulmagnion, Nils Charbonnel, Ingwill Wammer, Yorel Cayla, Maïssa Chahed.

Special thanks to Philippe Saglio, les Hôtels Costes, Romain Thomas, Alexandre Bernard, Olivia Bidou, Alain Bisotti, Les Hôtels Paris Rives Gauches, La Belle Juliette, Eric Bourquin, Ingvild Edvardsson & Amandine Vignon.

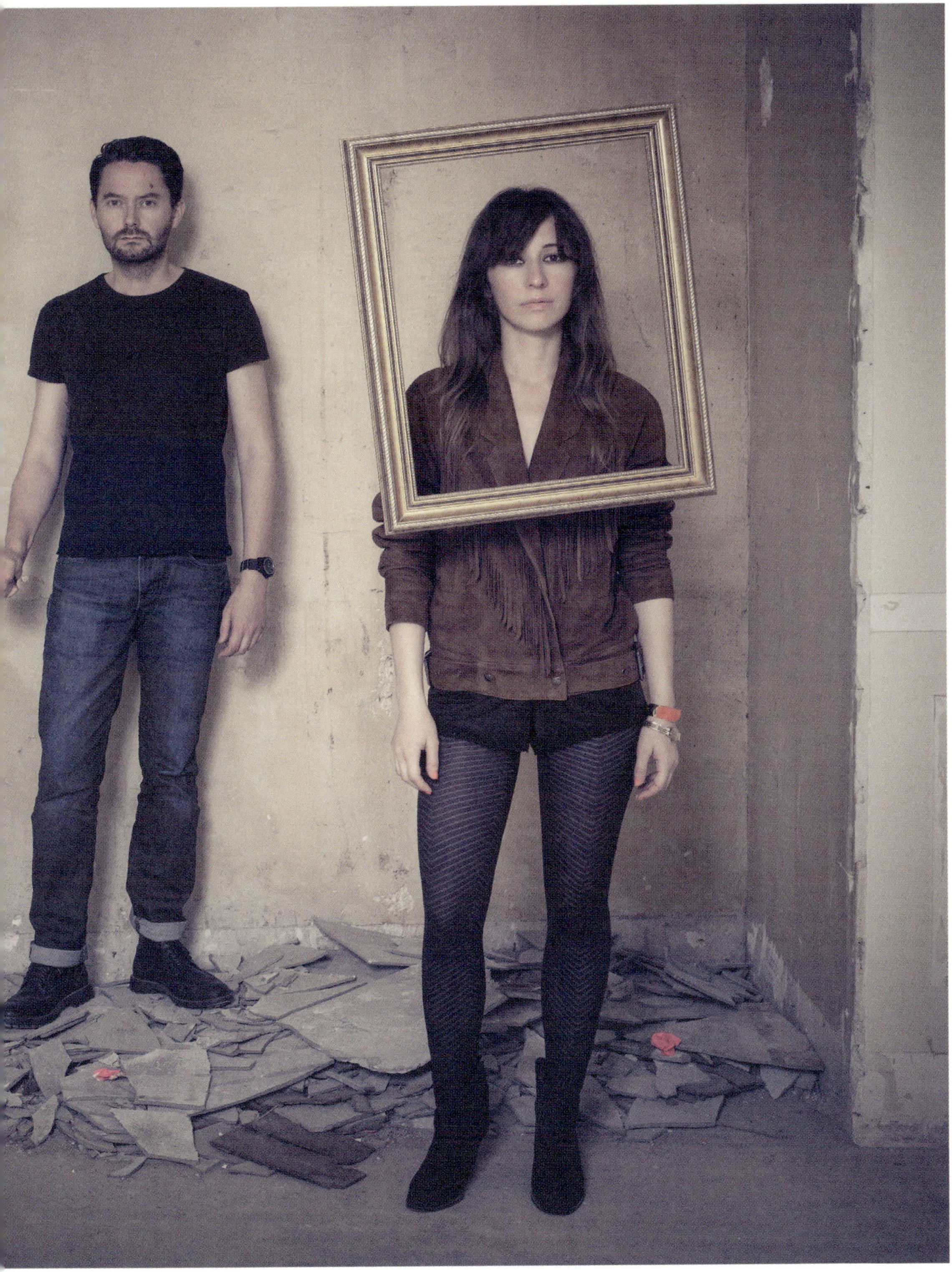

COLOPHON

Photography by **Marc Thirouin**

www.marcthirouin.com

Published by **New Heroes & Pioneers**
Models Cover are **Yorel Cayla & Maïssa Chahed**
Texts by **Amandine Vignon**
Photo assistant by Laura G.Berson (Paris)
& Frédéric Rougier (Oslo)
Post production by La French (re)touch

Co-edited by **Emma Hansson**
and Francois Le Bled

Creative Direction by **Jens Lennartsson**
Book design by **Lara Caputo**

Printed by ThePrintlink (Denmark)

FSC www.fsc.org MIX From responsible sources FSC® C107832

Legal deposit January 2015

ISBN 978-91-878150-4-1